Through the
NIGHT
SKY

CONTENTS

Into darkness 38–43
Happy New Year! 44–49
Signs in the stars 50–53
A journey to Earth 54–61
A visitor from above 62–67
Eyes to the sky 68–75
Our base in space 76–83
Seeing the solar system 84–91

NIGHT FLIGHT

As night falls over the countryside, a ghostly looking barn owl leaves its roost and sets off across the fields. Flying on silent wings, the owl's evening hunting trip is lit by the moon. By hunting at night, this beautiful bird does not have to compete with daytime fliers, such as kestrels and hawks.

Silent stalker

Superbly adapted to the dark, the barn owl uses its supersharp senses of hearing and sight to locate mice and voles. Soft feathers along its wings allow it to fly silently so it can listen for even the faintest sound of prey.

The barn owl spots a mouse...

...swoops low...

Barn owls can be seen near farms and woods.

A barn owl doesn't hoot— it screeches and hisses.

Mouse

Voles

Owl eyes ➤

Just like your ears, a barn owl's heart-shaped face collects sounds. The owl's ears are hidden under feathers, and one is slightly higher than the other to help pinpoint the tiniest of sounds.

...and grabs it with outstretched talons.

Owl eyes ➤

A barn owl's big eyes are essential for catching as much light as possible so it can see in the gloom. An owl can only look straight ahead, but it has a very flexible neck and can turn its head around and almost upside down.

Mealtime

Perched on a rock, the barn owl settles
down to enjoy its catch. It can't chew
its food into pieces, so it usually swallows
it whole. Any bits of fur and bones that
it can't digest are coughed up as
black pellets, revealing exactly
what the owl has eaten.

On a good night, a
barn owl can catch
four or five mice.

A lifelong bond

Barn owls build nests in holes in trees, in barns, and in nest boxes. A male and female pair up for life, using the same nest site every year. They usually lay two to three eggs, which hatch into hungry chicks that keep their parents busy hunting for food.

LIGHTING THE DARK

As night falls, darkness settles over the forest world. Even the brightest moonlight doesn't cut through the trees. Beneath the inky blackness of the night sky, the forest animals have developed ways of being able to see, and be seen, in the gloom.

Elk

Nighttime animals have especially keen senses of sight, hearing, and smell so they can find their way in the dark.

Bobcat

Nocturnal animals are animals that are mostly active at night.

Coyote

Black bear

Shine a light ➢

Some living things can make
their own light. This ability is called
bioluminescence. Among them
are deep-sea fish, squid, and even
sharks. In the forest, the most
famous light-producers are fireflies.

Firefly

Lightning bugs

If you see twinkling lights in the forest on a summer's night,
they could well be made by fireflies, also called lightning bugs.
Fireflies can make their own light, and switch it on and off
at will, like tiny flashlights. Different species of firefly create
different patterns of light as they fly through the night.
Some give out short flickers of light, with long gaps in
between. Others create a long-lasting glow.

Fireflies use their light to
attract mates so they can breed.
The different patterns allow male
and female fireflies from the same
species to recognize each other.

Dancing lights

Some species of firefly have an amazing talent. They can synchronize their flashing lights. That means they can turn them on and off in perfect unison, in short bursts. At certain times of the year, thousands of fireflies gather together for the mating season. A few begin flashing, then the others join in as the days pass. The result is a magical, glittering light show that shimmers through the night sky.

Most fireflies make yellow lights, but lights can also be green, blue, or orange.

Some types of forest fungi can also make their own light.

Clever chemicals ➢

Fireflies make light in the part of the body called the abdomen. Here, special cells contain chemicals that mix with oxygen to produce a glow. The fireflies can control the flow of oxygen into their bodies to switch the lights on and off.

Adult fireflies flash to attract mates. Firefly larvae also glow to warn predators that they taste horrible to eat.

SEEING WITH STARS

Human or animal—we are all influenced by the night sky. But one unlikely creature has an unusual, but very special, connection to it. During the day, the little dung beetle uses the position of the sun to help it travel in a straight line. At night though, when that's not an option, it needs something else to keep it on track.

Dung beetle

Dung beetles are incredibly strong. They can push dung balls 50 times their own weight.

Dung dependent ➤

The dung beetle collects the dung of
other animals to eat and feed its young.
However, competition from other dung beetles
is fierce, so it shapes the dung into balls and
rolls it away so other beetles can't steal it.

Dung beetles rely on the
dung of larger animals,
such as elephants.

Quick getaway ➤

It's vital that the dung beetle roll its
prize in a straight line. If not, it may
wander off course, back toward the
dung pile, where another beetle
could easily steal its precious ball.

Gazing at our galaxy

One of the most incredible sights in the night sky is the Milky Way—a beautiful, glowing band of light stretching across the sky. To us, the Milky Way is our home in space—an enormous galaxy containing our planet Earth, our solar system, and billions of stars. But to the dung beetle, it's the perfect solution to its problem.

A guiding light ➤

If there is no sun or moon to guide them, dung beetles use the light from the Milky Way to get their bearings, so they can push their balls of dung in a straight line.

The Milky Way

Galaxies are gigantic clusters of dust and gas that contain stars. The Milky Way is an enormous spiral, but, from Earth, it appears like a band across the sky. This is because we can only see part of one of its spiraling "arms."

The Milky Way contains at least 100 billion stars and is so big that light takes around 100,000 years to cross from one side to the other.

On cloudy nights, dung beetles can end up going around in circles.

A NIGHT OF FLOWERS

On the island of Madagascar, off the coast of Africa, giant baobab trees stand under the first storm of the season. As lightning streaks across the dark sky and rain beats down on the dusty ground, the trees drink in the water and prepare for the most enchanting night of the year.

Pollen →

Long-tongued
hawk moth

Blooming at dusk

After a few weeks of raging storms, the
rain stops and the baobabs shed their leaves
to save energy. In their place, the trees grow
strange, round pods. As the sun goes
down and dusk draws in, the pods crack
open to reveal a glimpse of bright
white flowers inside.

On the wind ➤

When the buds open, the smell
of the baobab's flowers is carried
on the warm wind. Drawn in by the
scent, animals from all around start to
gather and make their way to the tree.

Fluttering moths ➤

Giant night-flying hawk moths visit the
baobab's flowers to drink nectar—a sweet, sugary
liquid. Inside the flowers is a fine powder called pollen.
As the moths feed, specks of pollen stick to their bodies.
Then, when the moths fly from flower to flower,
they spread the pollen around the tree.

Flowers in the dark

Only once the sun has gone down and stars fill the sky will the baobab's flowers open fully. The moonlight illuminates the white petals so they stand out in the darkness. Guided by the flowers' scent, nocturnal lemurs climb the branches and giant fruit bats swarm around the tree.

Fruit bat

Night visitors ➤

Like the hawk moths, the bats and lemurs flit from flower to flower, drinking the nectar inside. As they press their noses between the petals, their faces become dusted with pollen. When they visit the next flower, they spread the pollen they are carrying on their fur.

Pollen

Lemur

The cycle goes on

As the sun starts to rise, the animals return to their roosts and dens to sleep, and the flowers begin to wilt. The baobab only blooms for one night a year, but the pollen the animals spread will help new seeds grow. In a few years' time—and with a little luck—these little seeds will grow into giant trees.

The brightest lights are brilliant yellows and greens.

HEAVENLY LIGHTS

In one of the most magical spectacles in nature, the night sky above the North and South poles fills with rippling curtains of light. Gorgeous greens, blues, reds, and purples swoop and sway, fold and unfold, in a dazzling display. This is called an aurora, and it's a sight that, once seen, you'll never forget.

From the sun ➤

For an aurora to appear, streams of particles
too small to see stream away from the sun.
They bump into gases in Earth's atmosphere and
magnetic field, creating a magnificent light show.
Auroras also happen on Jupiter and Saturn.

In Finnish myth, the lights were thought to be sparks that flew from the fur of fire foxes walking across the sky.

The Inuit people of the Arctic believe the lights are the spirits of the dead playing a strange ball game on the frozen snowfields in the sky.

A pod of whales feeds beneath the shimmering sky. Some ancient peoples thought the aurora was the blow of whales like these.

Northern light

Above the freezing waters of the Arctic Ocean,
an aurora makes the sky dance. Here, the aurora
is called the aurora borealis, or the northern lights.
Ancient peoples told many stories to explain this
mysterious display. In Roman myth, Aurora was
the goddess of dawn who rode across the
night sky in her chariot.

Up to 20,000 pairs of birds live
in an emperor penguin colony.

Penguin power

Under the dancing sky, emperor penguins
gather in masses. Emperor penguins are one
of the only animals built to withstand the
howling winds and freezing temperatures of
the Antarctic winter. They have thick feathers
and reserves of fat to help keep the cold at
bay, and when the temperature is at its
coldest, they huddle together for warmth.

Emperor penguins
are the largest type of
penguin, at more than
4ft (1.2m) tall.

To see the aurora at its best, you need a bright cloudless sky.

Southern lights

Meanwhile, at the other end of the Earth,
the aurora australis, or the southern lights,
stages another breathtaking show. However,
the best place to watch these lights is in
Antarctica during the bitter winter, making
it impossible for most people to
witness the aurora in its full glory.

Ancient peoples thought wolves howled at the moon, but howling is just a wolf's usual way of talking to the others in its pack.

THE MOON

Pitted with craters from crashing meteorites, the moon is a giant ball of rock in the sky. People have gazed on it for centuries, wondered about it, and worshiped it. It is our closest neighbor in space, and the only other place humans have visited. The moon orbits Earth, appearing—but only appearing—to change shape night to night. These shapes are known as the phases of the moon.

Moon shine ➤

Although the moon is the brightest
object in the night sky, it doesn't
make any light of its own. We can see
it because light from the sun falls
on it and is reflected back to Earth.

33

Magic of the moon

A gleaming full moon is an awe-inspiring sight. The moon has a strong pull on our planet, even though it's much smaller than Earth, and almost 239,000 miles (385,000 km) away. Take the tides, for example. Gravity from the moon and sun pull the water in Earth's oceans into a bulge, making the tides rise and fall. The moon also affects how animals behave.

Midnight feast ➤

Nightjars are small nocturnal birds that have large eyes for hunting prey in the dark. Scientists have found that on moonlit nights the birds spend much longer feeding because it's easier to see.

Nightjars snatch moths and other insects from the air.

European nightjar

A nightjar's journey
to Africa takes about
three months.

Nightjar navigation ➤

Every fall, nightjars migrate from Europe to Africa.
They seem to time their departure by the moon, setting off
on their long journey around 10 days after a full moon.

Lunar light

When you look up at the moon, does it seem to change shape on different days? The sun lights one side of the moon and, as the moon orbits the Earth, we see more or less of the lit side. So, in fact, the moon stays the same—what changes is the amount of the lit side we can see.

Changing shapes ➢

The different shapes of the moon we see are called phases.
It takes 29.5 days for the moon to go through these phases.
The cycle starts with a new moon, has a full moon in the
middle, and ends with a crescent moon.

Crescent
moon

Part of the moon is always
turned away from Earth—it's
called the far side, or "dark" side,
because we can never see it.

INTO DARKNESS

It's noon on a day like any other. The sun sits high in the sky, and people and animals are going about their normal routines. Suddenly, the world is plunged into darkness—without warning, day turns into night. The day has been interrupted by one of nature's greatest spectacles—a total solar eclipse.

Impalas

Hippopotamus

Bad omens ➤

In the past, people were terrified of eclipses because they had no way of understanding what caused them. Today though, eclipses are exciting events that people travel great distances to witness.

African
spoonbills

Zebra

Eclipses can affect
animal behavior in
surprising ways.

Hamerkop

Cast in shadow

The Earth and moon are constantly moving through space. Every so often, they line up perfectly so that the moon comes between the Earth and the sun. For a few minutes, the moon blocks out the sun's light, and darkness falls. This is a total eclipse. Even though the moon is 400 times smaller than the sun, it's around 400 times closer to Earth—making it capable of blocking out the sun's light completely.

Earth

Total eclipse ➤

A total solar eclipse happens somewhere on Earth usually about every 18 months. The moon appears as a black circle surrounded by a ring of white light. More often, the moon only covers part of the sun, giving a partial eclipse. This happens about twice a year.

Sun

Moon

Lunar eclipse ➤

Another type of eclipse—a lunar eclipse—happens when
the moon swings behind the Earth and into its shadow.
The moon doesn't give off its own light, and only appears
bright because it reflects light from the sun. During a lunar
eclipse, almost all the sun's light is blocked from reaching the
moon, making the moon appear dark red. This is because the
light it is lit by has passed through Earth's atmosphere.

Bats that roost in trees
are thought to come out
during a solar eclipse,
thinking it's nighttime.

When darkness comes

On Earth, the effects of the solar eclipse are astonishing. For
around 8 minutes, day turns to night, the temperature drops,
stars appear, and streetlights in cities flicker to life. Just as
amazing is the dramatic way in which animals react.

Because the moon's surface isn't perfectly smooth, small glimpses of sunlight peek out from around the moon.

Eclipse effects ➤

Scientists are fascinated by the effect an eclipse has on wildlife. But while many interesting sightings have occurred, the full effects of a solar eclipse on animals are still something of a mystery.

Animal antics

Famously, during an eclipse, many birds stop singing. Owls, on the other hand, start hooting, crickets chirp more, mosquitoes become more active, and hippos have been seen waking from their naps and wandering around confused and disturbed.

Fire dancing ➤

On Samoa, the New Year is welcomed in with a feast, songs, and a spectacular dance. Dancers twirl long, blazing sticks, throwing them high into the air and catching them with extraordinary skill.

HAPPY NEW YEAR!

It's midnight on December 31, and on the little island of Samoa in the Pacific, New Year's celebrations are in full swing. The Pacific islands of Tonga, Samoa, and Kiribati are the first places on Earth to welcome in the New Year.

The dance was
once performed by
warriors before they
went into battle.

Striking midnight

As midnight strikes in Samoa, it's only 10 in the morning on December 31 in London, England. When midnight comes, thousands of excited onlookers gather on the banks of the Thames River, ready for the evening's entertainment. As Big Ben bongs 12 times to ring in the New Year, the crowd counts down to an electrifying firework display.

Big Ben

Thousands of
flashes and bangs
light up the sky.

Happy New Year!

Perfect timing ➤

A year is how long it takes for Earth to orbit the
sun. As it travels, Earth spins on its axis. This means
that the sun shines on places facing it, giving daylight,
while places on the opposite side are in the dark. Because
of this, different places on Earth have different times.

Fatu Rock,
Tutuila Island

Last, but not least

The last places to greet the New Year are all the way over on the other side of the world, almost where we began. By the time it's 11 in the morning on January 1 in London, the clock is striking midnight on December 31 on the islands of American Samoa. To celebrate, there are countdown parties, church services, and hopes that the morning sky will be clear for the first spectacular sunrise of the year.

Full circle

Technically, Baker Island is the last place to welcome in the New Year, but no one lives there.

Despite their time difference, Samoa and American Samoa are just a short flight apart. People can start their New Year's celebrations in Samoa, hop on a plane, and celebrate all over again when they land.

Cassiopeia is named after a queen from Greek myth. It's made of five stars that form a "W." shape.

Shifting stars ➤

Throughout the year, the stars and constellations appear to turn and change position. However, it's actually the Earth that is moving and causing the stars to shift.

SIGNS IN THE STARS

For centuries, humans have gazed up at the stars, told stories, and formed imaginary shapes and patterns from them. These patterns have become known as constellations. There are 88 of them, and most are named after figures from mythology, objects, and animals.

North Star

Ursa Minor means
"smaller bear." It contains
the North Star, a star
that always points the
way North.

Draco is a large
constellation named after
a dragon from Greek
myth. Its "tail" curls
around Ursa Minor.

Look for the shape of a house
with a pointed roof. This is the
constellation of Cepheus. It is
named after King Cepheus,
Cassiopeia's husband.

Time and place ➤

The time of year, and where you
are in the world, determines
which constellations you can see.
The four constellations above
are only visible to people who
live in Earth's Northern Hemisphere
(the top half of the planet).

Centaurus is named after a mythical creature that has the head of a human and the body of a horse.

Crux, or the Southern Cross, is the smallest constellation in the sky. Look for a cross shape that is made of four stars.

Southern skies

On the other end of the world is Earth's Southern Hemisphere. Here, the constellations you can see are different from those in the North. The best time to spot them is between March and

Carina is named after part of
a legendary ship. It contains
the star Canopus, which is the
second brighest in the sky.

Canopus

Far, far away

From our viewpoint on Earth, the stars that make up the
constellations appear to be close together. But this is just
an illusion. In fact, they are separated from each
other by distances so huge they are almost
impossible to imagine.

Asteroid

A JOURNEY TO EARTH

A shooting star streaking across the night sky is an amazing sight. But what's just as amazing is knowing that many of these magical trails of light were once fragments of rock and metal called asteroids, which are leftovers from the formation of our solar system more than 4 billion years ago.

Meteoroid

Breaking away

There are millions of asteroids in the solar system, mostly floating between Mars and Jupiter. When asteroids smash into each other, smaller pieces of rock called meteoroids break away. These hurtle through space, sometimes toward Earth.

Asteroids range
from being hundreds
of miles across to the size
of a boulder. Anything
smaller is a meteoroid.

Streaks in the sky

When a meteoroid comes speeding into Earth's atmosphere, it burns up, creating a brilliant, glowing streak of light called a meteor. A meteor is what we call a shooting star. In fact, meteors have nothing to do with stars—they're just pieces of rock burning up and fading away.

Meteor showers ➤

Meteors fall to Earth every day, but sometimes,
lots fall at the same time. This is called a
meteor shower. A meteor shower occurs
when Earth passes through dust left behind
by a comet traveling around the sun.
It's like a fireworks display in the night sky.

A journey's end

Most meteors burn up in the atmosphere and vanish, but sometimes small pieces survive and crash to Earth as meteorites. After a long journey through space, all that is left of the once huge asteroid is a chunk of rock and a small crater.

Rare rocks ➤

Around 50,000 meteorites have been found on Earth. While most meteorites start off as asteroids, some are actually small pieces of Mars or the moon that were blasted off when they were struck by an asteroid, but these are very rare.

Many meteorites land in the ocean and vanish.

Meteorite

A scar in the Earth

Although meteorites are usually about the size of a fist, they strike the ground at such high speed, they leave bowl-shaped craters behind. Most craters wear away over time, but some of the bigger ones leave permanent marks in the Earth.

A VISITOR FROM ABOVE

Almost 2,000 years ago, on a quiet hilltop, Babylonian astronomers witnessed an amazing sight—a mysterious bright light in the night sky. As they watched in wonder, they were also puzzled as to what the light could be. Little did they know that this was not the first time this light had appeared, and it would not be the last...

A comet appears

The mysterious light appeared again and again during the centuries that followed. When it arrived, it appeared suddenly from out of nowhere, often causing fear and confusion. Soldiers fighting in the Battle of Hastings in 1066 thought the light was a falling star, when in fact, it was a comet, hurtling through space.

Icy visitors ➤

Comets aren't falling stars. They are pieces of ice, rock, dust, and gas that travel around the sun. From time to time, they swoop into the inner solar system and appear in the sky, only to vanish and continue on their way shortly after.

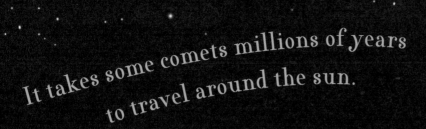

It takes some comets millions of years to travel around the sun.

Heating up ➤

For most of its journey, a comet is impossible to see. But as one comes near the sun, its heat melts the ice, and the gas and dust form a cloud around the comet. The solar wind (streams of particles from the sun) push the cloud into a long tail.

Until next time...

Comets have been seen for many, many years.
But it wasn't until a few hundred years ago that the
astronomer Edmond Halley figured out that many
of these sightings were the same comet returning
again and again. Thanks to Halley's calculations,
we now know when to expect this comet
to appear in the night sky again.

Halley's Comet

Halley saw the comet for himself
in 1682 and knew that it had last
appeared in 1607 and 1531. From these
dates, he realized that the comet came
into the inner solar system every
76 years or so, which is when it
could be seen from Earth.

Halley's comet was last visible in 1986, and will return again in 2062.

Halley died before he was proven right, but the comet was named Halley's Comet in his honor.

EYES TO THE SKY

In some far-flung corners of the world, away from cloudy skies and the bright lights of cities, astronomers gather in places called observatories to study the deep reaches of the universe. During the day, these observatories and their surrounding areas are still and quiet, but when the sun sets, they come to life as astronomers fire up their telescopes.

Seeing the starlight

Once the sun drops below the horizon, stars seem to flood the night sky. The human eye can see around 3,000 stars, and while this is an awe-inspiring sight, there are billions and billions more stars that we cannot see. Inside an observatory are powerful telescopes—machines that are able to reveal parts of the universe that we could never hope to see with our eyes alone.

Out in isolation ➤

Observatories are built in remote locations, far from the light and dust pollution found around cities. They are also usually built in deserts or high in the mountains, where the air is still, dry, and free from clouds—giving them the clearest, darkest skies, and the best possible view of the universe.

Through the lens

Telescopes can capture much more of the light that comes from space than our eyes can. They allow us to look far into the vast reaches of space, revealing detailed images and millions of objects that we would otherwise be unable to see. Among these spectacular sights are nebulas—incredible regions of space where stars are born.

So much more ➢

Ancient civilizations have gazed at the stars for generations. But the invention of the telescope revealed that as well as stars, planets, and moons, space is filled with twisting galaxies, exploding stars, black holes, nebulas, and so much more than we could have ever imagined.

The Eagle Nebula is an enormous nebula in the Milky Way. At its center is an area known as the Pillars of Creation.

Nebulas ➤

Stars are huge balls of gas that give off heat and light. They start off in gigantic clouds of glowing dust and gas called nebulas and form over the course of millions of years.

Pillars of Creation

Telescopes ➤

Telescopes work by capturing light from space and focusing it using a curved lens or mirror. Space telescopes are built using enormous mirrors. The bigger the mirror, the more light the telescope can gather.

73

The Pillars of Creation

At the center of the Eagle Nebula are three giant finger like columns that stretch out an unimaginable distance. They are called the Pillars of Creation because of the number of stars born inside them.

The Hubble

The Pillars of Creation were first photographed in 1995 using the Hubble Telescope, which was launched into Earth's orbit to get an even better view of space than is possible from Earth.

The Pillars of Creation are so far away that it takes 7,000 years for the light from there to reach us.

OUR BASE IN SPACE

High above the Earth flies a spacecraft the size of a football field, and the most ambitious space project in history. Since 2000, the International Space Station (ISS, for short) has been a home to different crews of astronauts and a giant science laboratory where they conduct research into the effects of travel in space. It is the biggest artificial object ever to orbit Earth, and can be seen as a bright light in the night sky.

Sunrise and sunset

The ISS zips through space at a speedy 4.8 miles (7.7 km) per second and only takes about 90 minutes to travel the whole way around the Earth. This means it completes a full trip around the planet 16 times a day. As a result, the astronauts on board are treated to 16 spectacular sunrises and sunsets.

Solar panels

Sun power ➤

All that sunlight is incredibly useful. Solar panels on the ISS harness the power of the sun's rays and turn them into electricity. This is used to power the station's systems and equipment.

The "Cupola," is a domed module on the ISS with stunning views from its seven windows.

On board the ISS

The first astronauts arrived on the ISS in November 2000, and many crews have lived on board since then. The astronauts live and work on the station for months or even years. Inside, the station is as big as a house, with five bedrooms, two bathrooms, and a gym.

Aurora

Lightning

City lights at night ➤

Astronauts aboard the ISS are kept busy, conducting scientific experiments, fixing equipment, and carrying out other missions. It's difficult and dangerous work, but it has many amazing perks. The astronauts get to experience the best view of Earth that a person can have—taking in the incredible sight of twinkling city lights, storms, and auroras below.

Other than the sun and moon, the ISS is the brightest thing in our sky. We can see it because sunlight bounces off it.

Passing overhead

The ISS orbits the Earth at a height of around 250 miles (400 km). While this is certainly a long way away, it's still close enough that the station is visible on a clear night. At this distance, the station will look like nothing more than a fast-moving star, but as it passes overhead, you'll be gazing up at one of humanity's greatest achievements.

The station travels on an arcing path as it makes its way across the night sky.

ISS

Spot the station

NASA (National Aeronautics and Space Administration) created a tool called "Spot The Station," which makes it easy for people to track the path of the ISS as it flies overhead. With its help, anyone can find when and where to look for it on its journey around the world.

The farther away you are from the bright lights of a city, the easier it is to see light from objects in space.

Our eyes in space ➤

Humans have been launching probes since the 1950s. Some probes are designed to land on or orbit around a particular planet or moon, while others fly past objects, recording information from a distance and sending it back to Earth.

The exact trajectory (path) a probe will travel is determined long before it is launched.

SEEING THE SOLAR SYSTEM

Much of what we know about space we know because of probes—unmanned spacecraft launched into space with special technology to analyze, photograph, and send data back to Earth. These robotic explorers have spent decades exploring the solar system and beyond, helping us to deepen our understanding of what mysteries lie in the far reaches of space.

The Red Planet

Aside from Earth, the planet we know most about
is Mars. Scientists have successfully sent robots to
explore the surface of Mars, and work is currently
underway to try to send astronauts there in the
future. Once a probe leaves Earth's atmosphere,
it will drift through the emptiness of space
for months before reaching Mars.

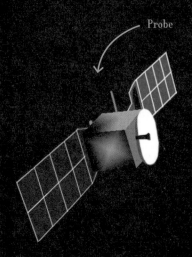

Probe

Mars is known as the
Red Planet because
the iron in its soil
and atmosphere
makes it look red.

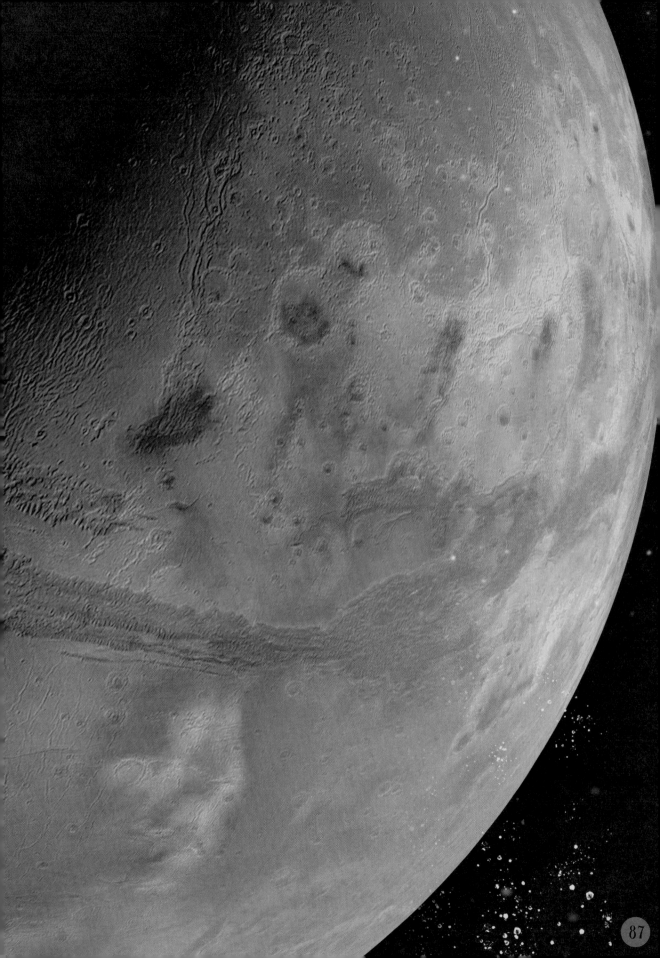

Jupiter has 79
moons, including one
called Ganymede,
which is bigger than
the planet Mercury.

King of the planets ➤

The largest planet in our solar system is Jupiter.
This giant ball of gas is so large that all the
other planets combined could fit inside it.
In 2011, NASA launched a probe called Juno
to Jupiter. After a five year journey, it entered
Jupiter's orbit and has been sending valuable
information back to Earth ever since.

The gas giants

Far beyond Mars lie the "gas giants" Jupiter and
Saturn. These enormous planets were first seen
in the night sky by ancient people, but thanks to
probes, we have been able to learn so much more
about them. Jupiter is famed for its size, and Saturn
is best known for its beautiful, dazzling rings.

The Pioneer 11
probe was the first
of many to travel
to Saturn in 1979.

Saturn's rings are made of billions of pieces of ice, rock, and dust.

Our place in space ➤

The solar system contains eight planets, around 170 moons, thousands of known comets, billions of asteroids, and at the center, one star (the sun), which everything else travels around.

The planets closest to the sun are Mercury and Venus.

Mercury is the smallest planet, and Venus is the hottest.

Mercury

Venus

Earth

Mars

Asteroid belt

The sun

Neptune

Uranus

Saturn

Jupiter

At the very edge of our solar system lies the Kuiper Belt, a vast region containing minor planets, such as Pluto, and millions of other rocky and icy objects.

What lies beyond?

The four planets closest to the sun, including Earth, are made of rock. The other four are made of gases and have an icy or rocky core.

Scientists have spent decades sending probes around the solar system to planets, moons, comets, asteroids, and more. But in 2012, human civilization took its first steps beyond, when—after a 35 year journey—the Voyager 1 probe reached the edge of the solar system and traveled beyond into interstellar space.

INDEX

Author Anita Ganeri
Illustrator Charlotte Pepper
US Editor Margaret Parrish
US Senior Editor Shannon Beatty
Senior Editor James Mitchem
Senior Art Editor Claire Patane
Additional Design Polly Appleton,
Eleanor Bates, Charlotte Milner
Managing Editor Penny Smith
Managing Art Editor Mabel Chan
Senior Production Editor Tony Phipps
Production Controller Inderjit Bhullar
Project Picture Researcher Sakshi Saluja
Jacket Designer Elle Ward
Jacket Coordinator Issy Walsh
Publishing Director Sarah Larter
Creative Director Helen Senior

First American Edition, 2020
Published in the United States by DK Publishing
1450 Broadway, Suite 801, New York, NY 10018

Copyright © 2020 Dorling Kindersley Limited
DK, a Division of Penguin Random House LLC
20 21 22 23 24 10 9 8 7 6 5 4 3 2 1
001-311363-Sep/2020

A catalog record for this book
is available from the Library of Congress.
ISBN 978-1-4654-8150-4

DK books are available at special discounts when purchased
in bulk for sales promotions, premiums, fund-raising, or educational use.
For details, contact: DK Publishing Special Markets,
1450 Broadway, Suite 801, New York, NY 10018
SpecialSales@dk.com

Printed and bound in China

For the curious
www.dk.com

About the author

Anita Ganeri is an award-winning
author of hundreds of children's
information books. Before working in
publishing, she studied languages
at the University of Cambridge.
Among other things, she writes the
best-selling *Horrible Geography* series,
and loves to travel to far-flung places
whenever she can. Her books for DK
include *The Atlas of Exploration*, *DK First
Atlas*, and *DK First Encyclopedia*.

About the illustrator

Charlotte Pepper graduated with a
degree in surface pattern design. Over
the last 20 years, her career has been
focused mainly within the greeting card
industry, but recently, she has branched
into book illustration. Charlotte loves
working on a variety of subjects, such
as quirky characters and landscapes.
Charlotte also illustrated DK's
Through the Animal Kingdom.

Acknowledgments

The publisher would like to thank the following for their kind permission to reproduce their photographs:

Key: a= above; b=below/bottom; c=center; f=far; l=left; r=right; t=top.

1 123RF.com: Boris Stromar / astrobobo (c). 2-3 Shutterstock: Red ivory. 2 123RF.com: Boris Stromar / astrobobo (cra). 3 Alamy Stock Photo: Sasa Kadrijevic (cra). 5 Alamy Stock Photo: David Brabiner (c). 6-7 Dreamstime.com: Rbiedermann (b). 8-9 Dreamstime.com: Rbiedermann (b). 10-11 Alamy Stock Photo: Bill Lea / Dembinsky Photo Associates (b). 10 Getty Images: David Q. Cavagnaro (cb). 11 123RF.com: Brandon Alms (crb); Steve Byland (ca). Getty Images: David Q. Cavagnaro (cb). 13 Alamy Stock Photo: Philip Silver (cr). 14-15 naturepl.com: Floris van Breugel. 14 Alamy Stock Photo: Jacek Nowak (bl). 15 Getty Images: Ali Majdfar (cr). 16-17 123RF.com: Samart Boonyang (t). 16 Dreamstime.com: Neal Cooper (clb); Duncan Noakes (b). 17 123RF.com: mhgallery (clb); Duncan Noakes (cl). Getty Images: Don Farrall / Photodisc (cl/Baby elephant). Alamy Stock Photo: Nature Picture Library (bc). 18-19 Shutterstock: Red ivory (t). 19 Alamy Stock Photo: Rolf Nussbaumer Photography (br). 24-25 Dreamstime.com: Paop (Tree). 24 Alamy Stock Photo: blickwinkel (cra); Rolf Nussbaumer Photography (cla, c). 25 Alamy Stock Photo: Image Professionals GmbH (cb); Rolf Nussbaumer Photography (tc, cr, crb). 26-27 123RF.com: Atiketta Sangasaeng. 28-29 123RF.com: Petri Jauhiainen. Dreamstime.com: Denis Belitskiy (cb/Background). 28 Alamy Stock Photo: National Geographic Image Collection (cb). Dreamstime.com: Fiona Ayerst (bl). 30-31 naturepl.com: Stefan Christmann. 30 Getty Images: David Tipling / Digital Vision (clb). Dreamstime.com: Kotomiti_okuma (fclb). 31 Getty Images: Frank Krahmer / Photographer's Choice RF (br). 32 Dorling Kindersley: Jerry Young (cb). Dreamstime.com: Chris Lorenz / Chrislorenz (cb/Wolf). 33 123RF.com: Boris Stromar / astrobobo (t). 34 Alamy Stock Photo: Saverio Gatto (b). 35 123RF.com: Boris Stromar / astrobobo (t). 36-37 Dreamstime.com: Nerijus Juras (b). 37 123RF.com: Boris Stromar / astrobobo (c). 38 Alamy Stock Photo: blickwinkel (cla). Dreamstime.com: Giampaolo Cianella (c, crb); Ecophoto (c/Hippo Lying); Sergey Uryadnikov (cr/Front); Mathias Sunke (cl). 39 Alamy Stock Photo: Jez Bennett (cl); Gallo Images (tr); Robertharding (c, cb); Anette Mossbacher (cr). Dreamstime.com: Darren Davis (b). 41 Dreamstime.com: Levgenii Tryfonov / Trifff (tr). 42 Alamy Stock Photo: blickwinkel (ca); Cultura Creative Ltd (cra). Dreamstime.com: Leonmaraisphoto (b). naturepl.com: Piotr Naskrecki (tc, tr). 43 Alamy Stock Photo: Jez Bennett (cr); Christopher Scott (cra/Zebra). Dreamstime.com: Patrice Correia (c, cl); Solarseven (tc); Ecophoto (cl/Hippo Lying); Mikelane45 (cra). naturepl.com: Piotr Naskrecki (tl). 44 123RF.com: rodho (tl). 44-45 Dreamstime.com: Grafistart (b). 46-47 123RF.com: Jaromír Chalabala (Westminster and Big Ben). Dreamstime.com: Jaromír Chalabala. 48-49 Dreamstime.com: Eddydegroot. 49 123RF.com: Boris Stromar / astrobobo (tc). 50-51 Alamy Stock Photo: David Perkins. 51 Alamy Stock Photo: Nat Chittamai (br). 52-53 Alamy Stock Photo: Media Drum World. 55 123RF.com: aicrovision. 56-57 123RF.com: Juan Gaertner (t). 58-59 Getty Images: Pete Saloutos. 60-61 123RF.com: siraphol. Dorling Kindersley: John Freeman / (t). 60 123RF.com: Sommai Larkjit (crb). Dorling Kindersley: Natural History Museum, London (crb/Pebbles). Dreamstime.com: PixelParticle (fbl). 61 Getty Images: This image is property of Picardo (cla). Dorling Kindersley: Natural History Museum, London (cb, crb). Dreamstime.com: PixelParticle (cb/kelp). 63 Dreamstime.com: Solarseven (ca). 64-65 Dreamstime.com: Sue Martin. 64 Dreamstime.com: Solarseven (cra). 66-67 123RF.com: Songquan Deng (Buildings). Dreamstime.com: Maxym022. 67 Dreamstime.com: Solarseven (ca). 68-69 Alamy Stock Photo: blickwinkel. 70-71 Alamy Stock Photo: Robertharding. 72-73 Alamy Stock Photo: Irina Dmitrienko. 74-75 Alamy Stock Photo: Alexandr Yurtchenko. 76-77 Alamy Stock Photo: Sasa Kadrijevic. 78-79 Dreamstime.com: Konstantin Shaklein. 80-81 Alamy Stock Photo: NASA Photo. Dreamstime.com: Mopic (Porthole). 82-83 Alamy Stock Photo: James Farley (b). 86-87 Dreamstime.com: Mr1805. 88-89 Alamy Stock Photo: Tristan3D

Cover images: Front: Getty Images: Daniel Parent crb

All other images © Dorling Kindersley
For further information see: www.dkimages.com

DK would like to thank

Marie Lorimer for indexing, Chris Oxlade for his scientific expertise, and Alexina Thielemans at Advocate-Art.